For my mother and father

IT BEGINS WITH FRIENDSHIP

A Fresh Approach to Prayer

Greg Friedman, O.F.M.

Nihil Obstat:
    Rev. Andre McGrath, O.F.M.
    Rev. John J. Jennings

Imprimi Potest:
    Rev. Jeremy Harrington, O.F.M.
    Provincial

Imprimatur:
    †James H. Garland
    Archdiocese of Cincinnati
    August 17, 1984

The *nihil obstat* and *imprimatur* are a declaration that a book or pamphlet is considered to be free from doctrinal or moral error. It is not implied that those who granted the *nihil obstat* and *imprimatur* agree with the contents, opinions or statements expressed.

Scripture texts used in this work are taken from *The New American Bible*, copyright © 1970, by the Confraternity of Christian Doctrine, Washington, D.C., and are used by permission of the copyright owner. All rights reserved.

Cover and book design by Julie Lonneman.

SBN 0-86716-038-1

©1984, Greg Friedman, O.F.M.
All rights reserved.
Printed in the U.S.A.

Contents

Introduction   1

1. Meet Your God
   The Foundation for Prayer   3

2. The Friendship Model
   Talking to God as Friend   15

3. 'We Need the Eggs'
   Friendship With a Very Quiet God   27

4. The Machine Ate My Quarter
   Getting Answers in Prayer   35

5. Nothing But 'I Love You'
   Prayer in the Tough Times   47

6. All Styles and Colors
   A Sampling of Ways to Pray   59

Epilogue   71

Introduction

"How can you tell someone else how to pray?" That was my friend's question when I told her I was going to write a book on prayer. And it is a good question.

Prayer is a very personal business. I often find it frustrating to read or hear how someone else prays—I guess because I've had so much trouble learning how to pray myself.

I remember telling my spiritual director in the seminary how depressed I felt as I looked around the chapel and saw everyone else praying. He simply said, "How do you know they're praying?" His answer made me stop and think. I realized I should stop *comparing* my praying to someone else's and begin praying *my* prayer. No one else's prayer can be my prayer; I've got to discover my own.

As I reflect on those words I realize I may have just wiped out the reason for writing this book! And I certainly don't want to do that. Because true as it is that prayer is a very personal business, it is also true that we can learn a lot about prayer from others.

My own ability to pray has grown as I have read the Scriptures, the lives of the saints and other masters of the spiritual life; talked with friends; shared prayer with others; and, of course, *prayed*.

I offer you this book in that same spirit. It certainly isn't the last word on prayer, nor does it claim to be an in-depth, scholarly treatment. Rather, it's some of the things I would say to you about prayer if we were talking together about what is most important in our lives: our deepest needs and feelings, what makes us laugh and cry, the times we've tried to love and be loved—in short, the moments where God is breaking into our lives. For I believe those moments can teach us a lot about prayer.

If you're like me you will probably experience some frustration as you read this book. You may wonder, "Why doesn't he tell me the *secret*? How *do* you pray?"

If that question comes to mind—great! You're on the right track. We are all looking for "the secret" to praying. But I warn you at the beginning: You won't find it *here*. That's because you already possess it! It is *within you*, in the secret place where you meet God. I'm writing this book to encourage you—and me—to keep discovering that secret—over and over again—for all of our lives.

1. Meet Your God
The Foundation for Prayer

The movie *1776* usually is shown on television around the 4th of July each year. It's the story of how the Declaration of Independence was written, and the central character is John Adams. In one scene, near the end of the story, Adams is all alone. His friends in the Continental Congress are having a tough time getting the votes for independence from England. The glorious goal seems about to fail. Standing by himself in the congressional chamber, Adams sings, "Is anybody there? Does anybody care?"

Those words are almost a prayer! And, indeed, they make a good place to start talking about prayer. We all know prayer has something to do with God—but *Is anybody there? Does anybody care?* These are realistic questions. Today, in our culture and times, belief in God isn't always as easy as it was for people of earlier generations.

There's a marvelous series of fantasy books by Stephen R. Donaldson entitled *The Chronicles of Thomas Covenant the Unbeliever*. The hero of the series is a contemporary man, Thomas Covenant, who suffers from Hansen's Disease (formerly known as *leprosy*). When he is transported into a magical land where reality is quite different and where a great struggle between good and evil is taking place, Covenant thinks he's dreaming and refuses to believe the land is real. If he puts faith in what may only be a dream, he fears he will wake to find his "real," disease-filled life even more full of pain and suffering.

Like Thomas Covenant, we are all skeptics about what lies outside of our everyday experience. Science has trained us to be skeptical. What an embarrassment if we put faith in something that turns out to be fake! We look for proofs; we want to know if "it's for real."

The Struggle to Believe

That kind of struggle is a large part of wrestling with the question of God. Do I want to believe? What will my friends think? Will I look foolish if I put my faith in something that can't be seen? And why should I believe? Isn't the world around me enough?

Those are the questions you and I are born with. We can't escape them. And once we are old enough to begin relating to the world around us, those questions cry out for answers. Thomas Covenant asks them on almost every page. And yet, gradually, through his struggles, Thomas Covenant discovers some answers. He discovers *faith*.

Faith comes in such mysterious ways that we may not recognize it, or we may mistake it for something else. As we grow up most of us *learn about* faith from the beliefs and practices of the people around us—until the time when we can begin believing on our own.

It was that way for me. I grew up in a home where God was part of our family life. My parents prayed with me as a child and took me to church. They talked about God and helped me to make a space for God in my life. I still treasure these memories—like the time my Dad took me to spend an hour in church on Holy Thursday evening. I knew this was a special thing to do, out of the ordinary. I'm sure I didn't fully understand why.

Only gradually did I come to a time in my life when I could *choose* to believe—not because I was forced to by my parents or teachers, but because I wanted to. That choice wasn't all at once—in some dramatic conversion experience. No, it came little by little. And faith remains a struggle; just because I believed in something 10 years ago doesn't mean I'm off the hook *today*. I still have to choose!

Perhaps it's different for you. Maybe you first came to faith from a friend who shared a belief in God with you. Or maybe you learned about God all at once in a moment of deep hurt or tragedy—or a time of special joy. Or a moment of wonder—a spectacular sunset or the power of ocean waves crashing on the shore—may have brought you to a special awareness of God's presence.

No matter how it got there, I suspect there is something within you that we can call faith. You are after all reading this book, a book about prayer. We might not know the who's and what's and why's, but we all sense that the answer to our opening question, *Is anybody there?*, is *yes*!

Faith Means We Have Worth

But does it make a difference? Is it worth putting faith in some*one* being there? *Does anybody care?* In the theater piece *Mass*, by Leonard Bernstein and Stephen

Schwartz, one of the young "street people" sings, "I'll believe in 20 gods if they'll believe in me."

Believing in God is linked to believing in ourselves. Do we have a value? Are we worth anything in this world? Or are we, as another contemporary song proposes, "dust in the wind"?

Some years ago I met Father Dave Garrick who introduced me to the art of storytelling. He told me a story from the Bible that has a lot to do with faith, struggle and personal identity, the story of Jacob wrestling with the angel in Genesis 32:23-33.

The story is a simple one. Jacob is on his way home after years of absence. He fears that his brother Esau may be coming to do battle with him, since years before Jacob had cheated his brother. In the night, as Jacob is encamped all alone, a stranger appears and begins wrestling with him. The struggle goes on for hours, and as daybreak comes Jacob is defeating his attacker. Then the stranger strikes a paralyzing blow to Jacob's hip. Jacob still has him in a stranglehold, however, and the stranger begs to be released. But Jacob says, "I will not let you go until you bless me." "What is your name?" the man asks. He answers, "Jacob." Then the man says, "You shall no longer be spoken of as Jacob, but as Israel, because you have contended with divine and human beings and have prevailed." Jacob then asks him, "Do tell me your name, please." He answers, "Why should you want to know my name?" With that, he bids him farewell.

Jacob gives the place a symbolic name, *Peniel* ("the face of God"), thus indicating his belief that it was a messenger of God, come in human form, who struggled with him in the night.

As Father Garrick explains the story, it is a tale of finding an identity out of struggle. Jacob's wrestling match is, of course, with God. God lets that secret out in the new name for Jacob—*Israel*, "he who struggled with God." But notice that the stranger (God) is reluctant to give *his* name. Instead, it is out of the struggle, out of the wrestling, that Jacob comes to know God. And in the course of that discovery, Jacob also comes to know himself.

What a great story! And how true to the way our lives unfold. Out of our questions, out of our struggles, we discover not only who *we* are, but who our God is as well.

Faith *Is* the Struggle

The *search*, the *journey*, the *quest*—all these words describe faith, or at least a part of what believing is all about. That's because even the struggle to believe shows we have faith. I believe that struggle is part of what it means to be human, a seed planted there by God. You know that a seed, no matter how you plant it, will discover the direction of the air and sunlight and push its shoot that way. Faith is something like that.

We can have faith in "something," perhaps in a vague feeling that the world will turn out all right, that the universe is a friendly place. And yet, as human beings we need more. Somewhere at the heart of us, this faith-struggle turns to search for a Someone.

Our Images of God

Like Jacob, our wrestling becomes personal. *Is anybody there? Does anybody care?* Sooner or later, we have to confront a personal God. For most of us, this encounter comes about because the people who give us life and nurture us help to shape our searching. Our images of God are based on the people we know. I believe this happens because that's the way we're created to begin with. The seed struggling to believe, planted in us by God, looks for the air and light, and discovers them in the people around us.

Think for a moment about God. What picture comes to your mind? Do you envision a particular image? Is there a face? A feeling? Words or music? Let your mind travel until it comes to rest in the image that most says *God* to you. Then reflect for a moment: Where does this image come from? When do you first remember having it? Has it been a part of you for a long time? Has it ever changed, and if so, what caused the change?

Those questions might reveal a rich treasury of stories and images. There also might be more than one picture or feeling—and that's fine! When I begin reflecting on God, certain familiar, friendly stories come to mind.

When I think of God as creator, I envision the God of the Genesis story (Genesis 2:4b-11) who planted a garden and made things grow—including the first human beings. In my scene the figure of God looks a lot like my Italian grandfather, who grew tomatoes in our backyard when I was little. He'd putter around in frumpy clothes and an old hat. (And here my image begins to look a bit like Marlon Brando in the famous scene from *The Godfather* where the old godfather is near death, playing with his grandson in the garden.)

My grandfather was never much of a success as a gardener, but if you remember the story from Genesis, God the creator had a little trouble with his plants, too! The first human being was unhappy and needed further care and even some "pruning." And in the end, the story was a sad one, the story of sin.

I remember, though, a marvelous thing that happened one spring. A renovation took place. In a narrow strip of ground where my grandfather had planted tomatoes the year before, cement was poured to make a wider driveway for the family car. I guess it said something about the confidence my grandmother had in his gardening. But then came the miracle: Under a spigot sticking out of the house, where water dripped into a crack in the concrete, a tomato plant sprouted! It grew and bore fruit! To this day I don't know how it happened, but the memory is part of my image. And when I think of God and the garden I also remember that surprising things can happen.

That story isn't my only God-story or my only image of God. But I relate it to help you see where our images of God may begin—in the familiar faces around us as we are growing up; in the stories we read in the Bible; in our experience of wonder; and even in the popular culture.

Outgrowing Our Images of God

God is my friend, not a mosaic on a church wall or a picture in the family Bible. Like a relationship with any friend, I will relate to God in part through the way I envision God, through the image that I hold in my heart. My prayer will take shape around that image.

But because relationships work two ways, God also plays a part in the process of prayer. I believe that God is at work in my life, loving me and gifting me in ways that help me to grow. Like any friend, I learn who God is through this process.

With both avenues of communication at work, my image of God won't remain the same. It can—and must—change as I grow and change through life. New experiences and new people help that process.

One reason our images of God must change is that we often outgrow one way of looking at God. My picture of my grandfather puttering in the garden was a friendly, warm, nurturing image. But my grandfather didn't have all the answers for my growing up. I can remember him sitting on the porch, shrugging his shoulders in a tired way as life went on. Meanwhile I was discovering new things that he'd never seen.

And so my image of God changed. It had to. Any one picture of God would be stifling, because the reality of God is so much fuller. God isn't confined to just my image or picture; God isn't limited to my personal world.

That may come as a relief, especially if the image I've just used—that of a kindly grandfather—does not appeal to you. Your experience of father or grandfather may not be a pleasant one, thus using this image to help picture God may call up memories that are painful and certainly not helpful.

My "grandfather" image of God may work for me at one time in my life and not in another; it may not work for you at all. That's not because this image is wrong; it just does not express fully what is, after all, an *inexpressible* mystery—God.

False Images of God

But there are images of God which are simply wrong. (And there are people who hang onto them long after they should be able to know better.) For instance, the images of God as a harsh father or cruel judge; as an impersonal watchmaker who started the world going and sits back disinterestedly while it ticks along; as a vending machine who gives out goodies when I put in enough change. Some of these images may have started out as innocent stories of childhood, but we can see how they end up limiting the possibilities of growing in faith.

An adult whose image of God is a harsh father might live in fear that God is waiting to catch every little fault or failing. A person with a "vending machine" God might expect "rewards" for good deeds done or quick answers to prayers. (One way this harmful image of God is promoted is by those who pass around "chain letter" prayers that promise sure answers if prayed in a certain way.)

God is so much more than those faulty images! And God, if we take the chance and allow it, will break into our small world and reveal a new mystery.

Is anybody there? Does anybody care? As we've seen in this first chapter, those questions are the place we begin our search for God. They are the questions that also help us to understand ourselves as we come to know God. But they are also questions which continue to come. The answers we discover—our images of God—need to be examined as we grow and change. We may find the need to ask the questions again—and again!

If it seems a lot more complicated than when we began, hang on! The exciting part of the mystery of believing is that God comes in ways that are sometimes familiar, sometimes surprising, and sometimes frustrating. We will explore these in the rest of this book.

Stop to Reflect

What does *faith* mean to you?

Who are the people who have shared their belief with you?

Are there any special events—sad, happy, wondrous—which have helped you understand who God is?

What is your image of God today?

Has your picture of God ever changed?

Something to Try

Think back. What picture of God did you have as a small child? On paper, sketch or describe who God was to you then. Next, recall when that image changed—if it has. Again, describe the change (or perhaps how the original image is different). You might want to "chart" the changes over the years of your life. Ask a friend to do the same. Then discuss the similarities and differences you each find in your images of God.

Take Time to Pray

Here are some Scripture passages which suggest different images of God people have found helpful. Select one, read it and then spend some time speaking to God in your own words, making use of the image

you picked.
> Psalm 23 (shepherd)
> Psalm 31:2-4 (rock)
> Psalm 42:2-9 (water)
> Psalm 80:9-20 (gardener)
> Psalm 91:1-5 (bird)
> Isaiah 46:3-4 (mother)

2. The Friendship Model
Talking to God as Friend

Sitting alone on a Saturday night isn't usually my idea of fun. Weekends are a busy time for priests, and I can appreciate a quiet evening alone now and then. But I do look forward to time spent with special friends. When I have an "empty" evening to fill, I pick up the phone to call one of them. But it occasionally happens that, one unanswered ring after another, there's no one home. Then I can begin to feel pretty lonely.

That tug of loneliness is just one of the ways I know that friendship is an important—even crucial—part of life. I remember when someone first befriended me in a special way. My life changed so much! I felt worthwhile to someone else in a way I'd never felt before. There was someone who was interested in my thoughts about art, God, books and living. I wanted to know what my friend thought and to discover the unique features that made my friend stand out from others.

In the first chapter we looked at the struggle that's inside each of us, the struggle to know ourselves and our place in the world. I believe that need to search is planted there by God and is part of how we are to discover God. The wonderful mystery of how friendship changes our lives is another gift of God. It, too, becomes an important part of learning who God is for us.

Getting to Know God—Not So Easy!

A fellow Franciscan priest once said that the Bible is nothing more than the story of God saying, "I love you," to the whole human race—and what we have said in response. I think that's a good way to look at the history of God's relationship with the human family and with each of us. It's a story of friendship.

Throughout the pages of the Bible we can see a real friendship developing. Sometimes things get pretty rocky! God's people don't always appreciate what God is doing for them—or even the fact that friendship is being offered!

But part of that misunderstanding wasn't the fault of those Old Testament folks. After all, think of the confusion and misunderstandings that come when you are first trying to be friends with someone—especially someone you've admired "from afar" for a while, someone everyone looks up to. I have a friend who is a well-known author. For a long time I wanted to get to know him and, eventually, we became friends. But even after that happened I would still get nervous—wondering if he really liked me, or if I was just a bother!

Transfer that set of confusing feelings to the relationship between God and the people of Israel. Like all their neighbors in the ancient Near Eastern world, they shared certain ideas about divine beings. Part of their belief was in the awesomeness of God.

You can picture the scene at Mt. Sinai, the scene depicted in the movie *The Ten Commandments*: a vast mountain with lightning, thunder and smoke issuing from its summit. There was a great distance between God and human beings.

In fact, the biblical Book of Exodus, which gives us that picture of Mt. Sinai, describes the feelings of the people who went there to make a covenant with God and receive the 10 Commandments of the Law: They were afraid! They didn't want to see God face to face. They believed, like all the peoples of that time, that to do so meant death!

That conviction is captured in one scene between God and Moses. God invites Moses to come up on the mountain to witness the divine glory—a sort of special favor because Moses was a close friend of God. But the Lord first warns Moses:

> "…My face you cannot see, for no man sees me and still lives. Here…is a place near me where you shall station yourself on the rock. When my glory passes I will set you in the hollow of the rock and will cover you with my hand until I have passed by. Then I will remove my hand, so that you may see my back; but my face is not to be seen."
> (Exodus 33:20-23)

The story seems to imply that seeing God's back is just as good—and a lot safer! It reminds us that a relationship with God, as with human friends, can be scary, can have times when we sort of "back around" each other until we get acquainted!

The Old Testament shows us a *developing* friendship. That Exodus experience is only part of the story and, as time went on, people came to know God in many different ways. Yet Moses' story reminds us that knowing God isn't easy. Sometimes it seems there's a big stretch of universe between us and God. The author of the First Letter of John said it well: "No one has ever seen God" (1 John 4:12).

Reaching for the Unreachable

No matter how much we learn about God, there is always that note of mystery. Even if we modern folks no longer fear being struck dead by a face-to-face meeting with God, we know that God is bigger than we are! There's no way a human mind can ever completely get a hold on who God is. One of the greatest thinkers in the Church's history, St. Thomas Aquinas, wrote that when it comes to describing God about the best we can do is say what God is *not*. Any other way falls short, since God is always more than we can grasp!

This experience of dealing with the mystery of God is somewhat like trying to grasp the "bigness" of the universe. Remember those textbook explanations of the size of the solar system—if the sun is a beach ball sitting in the middle of a cornfield, the earth is a pea so many miles away? Well, when I hear that example, I get the picture. But when Carl Sagan starts describing the "billions and billions" of solar systems that make up the vast universe—I get a headache! I'd much rather retreat to the fantasy world of *Star Trek* and let Mr. Scott's warp drive take over!

And yet we cannot escape from the mystery of God. We must "befriend" it.

Befriending the Mystery

Just as the Exodus story of Sinai alerts us to the "distance" between us and God, a story from the New Testament, from the Gospel of John, bridges that distance. In chapters 13—17 we read about what Jesus did at the Last Supper, the night before he died. I think Jesus knew he was about to die, and that fact makes his words there all the more special—after all, we treasure a person's dying words.

In that section of John's Gospel Jesus shares with his disciples his feelings of closeness to them: "I call you friends," he says (John 15:15). He also explains to them that his friendship with them is also friendship with the Father, who sent Jesus: "Whoever has seen me has seen the Father" (14:9).

These parting words from Jesus to his friends contain a truth that is absolutely crucial for us. For they show us that, in Jesus, we have a way to come to know God that the Old Testament people could not imagine. In Jesus, God has come to meet us personally, to befriend us in a way that is no longer frightening or distant. Instead of the awesome glory not to be seen face to face, he is our friend, sitting across from us at a dinner table, telling us how much he cares.

This truth is the heart of Christianity. It is why Jesus is more for us than just a great teacher who lived a long time ago, a figure of history or a very holy person. He is, as he tells us in that same section of John's Gospel, "the way, and the truth, and the life" (14:6).

Jesus *is* the way we come to know the mystery of God, because as *both* God and human, he is our meeting-point with the mystery. It's what the author of the First Letter of John and his community were trying to say in these words:

> This is what we proclaim to you:
> what was from the beginning,
> what we have heard,
> what we have seen with our eyes,
> what we have looked upon
> and our hands have touched—
> we speak of the word of life.
> (This life became visible;
> we have seen and bear witness to it....)
> (1 John 1:1-2)

For those early Christians and for those who have come after them down through the centuries, Jesus is God visible in a way that we can understand. Jesus teaches us that the mystery itself is friendly, gracious and loving. And when we begin to pray, it is no longer to a vast, unfathomable and sometimes forbidding mystery; it is to a friend.

Getting the Language of Prayer Straight

With that basic truth as our foundation, we can go on to talk about prayer in terms of talking to a friend. But how does our trinitarian notion of God fit in here? Who is my friend? Whom do I pray to? Jesus? God the Father? The Holy Spirit?

We know that Jesus prayed to the Father (and encouraged us to do the same). And yet when the Church prays—for example in the prayers at Mass—it chooses a variety of ways to address the mystery of God. Many prayers are prayed "to the Father, through the Son, and in the Holy Spirit." But

Christians have also found it helpful to pray to Jesus or to the Holy Spirit.

Through the rest of this book I will be developing the "friendship model" as a way of prayer, a way of relating to the mystery. How I address that friendly mystery may vary, just as the Church's prayers vary. At times I may choose to pray to God as friend, without specifying a particular Person of the Trinity; other times I may want to center in on Jesus, the Father or the Spirit. I invite you to "try on" the language of prayer that feels best to you.

Prayer: The Friendship Model

Let's begin by looking at some of the things we know about friendship and seeing how they can help us describe our relationship with God:

Caring. A friend loves and cares enough to go out of the way to help. Such caring may come in the form of a phone call when it seems like my world is falling apart—or when it *isn't* and I need to celebrate. It can be disguised as a can of chocolate chip cookies or a hot dish from a neighbor to a mom with three kids down with the chicken pox and a stopped-up kitchen sink.

Challenge. A friend helps me to step out of the little world I build around myself. I learn to think about someone else for a while instead of myself. Friendship moves people to do unselfish, even heroic things: a midnight rush to the hospital, a weekend of babysitting, a risk to overcome years of fears and say, "I love you."

Understanding. A friend gives me back myself in a new way. Who else knows I'm a fanatic *Star Trek* fan and can recite for me Mr. Spock's most famous lines? Who else can listen to my inside jokes and not need them explained? Who else can throw me the lifeline of a knowing wink, a "you-can-do-it" nod when I am otherwise drowning in a sea of misunderstanding?

Space to grow. A friend gives the gifts of silence, time and distance, of creative space in my life which may or may not need to be filled with anything. It's a "growing space" in which to plant creative ideas, to survey my life and recover from failures, to just sigh away a mountain of troubles for a moment or two. Friendship offers presence—and when it comes without words it is precious indeed.

The door to prayer can swing open when I begin to apply the above expectations about friendship to my relationship with God.

God cares. I often find it easiest to pray when I have spent an evening with warm, caring friends. I begin by thanking the Lord for these special gifts in my life. I remind myself that their love *is* God's way of loving me. I may want to picture the Lord as part of the conversation with a friend, sitting in, enjoying the laughter and the tears which grace friendship.

God challenges. Just as human friends challenge me to grow, I can experience challenge from God. God's Word in Scripture is often a challenge for me. Take for instance the story of the rich young man. Jesus "looked at him with love" and then went on to offer a real challenge, "Sell what you have and give to the poor....Come and follow me" (Mark 10:21). My prayer might begin as a meditation on this or another story where I can hear the Lord asking me to leave behind some habit or possession to which I have been clinging and simply to follow, in a response of love.

God understands. And there are days when I just

want to be understood. Maybe a particular day has been a struggle to untangle some complicated emotions. I wonder if anyone can *really* know me. My prayer at such a moment may be a rush of tears. St. Therese of Lisieux, the Little Flower, said it this way: "I just say what I want to say to God quite simply and he never fails to understand."

God provides us space to grow. I experience that "growing space" at the end of the day when I let the dark surround me. In that silent space I can take the opportunity to meet God as I would a friend—and say what needs to be said.

Let me share with you a poem I wrote as part of a prayer experience. It captures some of the ways I have felt cared for, challenged, understood and gifted with the space to discover God:

> Silent Walker,
> You hear my anguished cries
>   in nightspaces of lonely wanting.
> You are the patient surprise
>   which borders my selfseeking.
> You are the truth of how we touch,
>   the only answer to our common pain.
> You are the flavor of my celebrating,
>   the wild, freeing, playful cause to laugh.
> You are tearful thanks
>   when I am lifted into true caring.
> You are innocent question-eyes
>   to re-create the child in me too.
> You are love given away
>   in some heedless gift of self.
> You are age-long faithful presence
>   always with us,
>   with us in the flesh-formed

oneness of this walk together.

This chapter began with an unanswered phone call to a friend. That lonely sound can make us wonder if we are truly alone in the world. I know I'm not, for as soon as I stop to think, I remember the people out there who love me, my friends who have gifted me with their love. And, as we've seen in this chapter, friendship can teach us a lot about relating to God.

In fact, it was the gift of friendship between One named Jesus and the scraggly band of men and women who walked the dusty roads of Galilee with him that showed the human race that the unfathomable mystery of God was indeed friendly. Because of Jesus, we can approach God with a new language, the language of friendship.

But just as human friendships are often a struggle, so it is with our relationship with God. I'm still struggling to be a friend to my friends. I'm still struggling to pray! Some days I think that struggle is an awful lot of work. Some days I'm lifted up by the power of love. But in prayer, as in any friendship, there are those lonely Saturday nights when the phone rings and rings—and no one answers. Those times can raise questions for us. In the next chapter I'd like to talk about some of those questions.

Stop to Reflect

What comes to mind when you hear the word *friendship*?

Can you think of or describe a particularly lonely time in your life?

Has your idea of God ever seemed overwhelming or frightening?

What does Jesus mean to you?

How do you relate human friendship and friendship with God?

Something to Try

This chapter listed some of the qualities of human friendship. Look back over the list and think of other qualities that friends bring into your life. Make your own list based on experiences from your own life and then...

Take Time to Pray

...Use your list as a preparation for prayer. One by one, look over the qualities you have written down. Think of examples from Scripture—especially the Gospels—which might describe how God fullfills each quality. Then allow your thoughts and reflections to lead into prayer.

3. 'We Need the Eggs'
Friendship With a Very Quiet God

In *Annie Hall* director Woody Allen tells the story of a relationship between two people—a relationship filled with happiness, complications, pain and eventually the sadness of saying good-bye. At the end of the movie Allen comes on the screen to tell a joke which, he says, sums up his feelings about relationships.

The joke is about a man who goes to see a psychiatrist. "The problem," the man says, "is my brother. He thinks he's a chicken!"

"That's terrible," the doctor responds. "You ought to get him some professional help."

"We thought about that," the man replies, "but, frankly, we need the eggs."

Woody Allen goes on to explain that relationships are like that. They are full of complications, ups and downs, sorrows and joys. Why do we keep getting into them? Frankly, we need the eggs!

A few years ago some friends (who, like me, are Woody Allen fans) gave me a T-shirt bearing the words, *We need the eggs*. These friends accept me as I am—with my good qualities and bad. Their gift says a lot about the mystery of human relationships.

But what about that lonely ringing of the telephone on a Saturday night? When I feel frustrated and lonely, like Woody Allen I ask myself: Why do I get into relationships? Why do I keep looking for friendship and love? Is it worth it?

It can be the same with prayer! And that is what this chapter is all about—the feeling that, when I pray, there seems to be no one home on the other end! My faith may tell me otherwise, but I still must deal with the fact that God *seems* pretty silent a lot of the time!

What can I do when God is so quiet? I still feel the need, in faith, to pray. I still feel drawn out of myself to the great mystery of the Someone who calls me in love. I can only answer as Woody Allen does: *We need the eggs!* Which is another way of saying that loving God involves me deeper in mystery.

Entering Into Mystery

I used to think that calling something "a mystery" was a cop-out—a way of getting around an idea that couldn't be explained. A lot of our "God ideas" were called *mysteries* when I was in grade school. How could there be three persons in one God? How could God be everywhere? What does "eternal" mean? Anything Sister or Father couldn't explain was labeled *mystery*—and that ended the discussion.

It wasn't until much later that I came to another appreciation of mystery. One modern philosopher, Gabriel Marcel, saw a mystery not as a problem to be figured out—like changing the tire on a car—but rather as a rich reality we will never exhaust.

This way of looking at mystery shifts the focus from the problem that can't be explained to the challenge to keep exploring.

A concrete understanding of this approach to *mystery* comes from my experience of backpacking in the mountains. One marvelous part of mountain climbing is that the beauty of a mountain is different at every hour of the day, from every angle. No one view exhausts its grandeur.

There's a mountain in the Smokies called Mt. Le Conte. The first time I climbed to the top of this peak, in 1983, I met a remarkable woman, Gracie McNicol. She began climbing Mt. Le Conte in her 60's and had just ridden horseback up the mountain on her 239th trip—at age 91!

For Gracie—despite her age and her doctor's order to switch from hiking to horseback riding—that mountain certainly wasn't a problem. It was an ever-changing, ever-rich mystery to be discovered anew each time she made the trip to the summit.

Seeing a mountain as a mystery helps me to appreciate the richness of creation; talking about God as *mystery* clues me in to the richness that I can discover, even in the frustrating silence of God.

Let's explore that mystery a bit.

Probing the Silence of God

So often God seems to be silent. We pray and pray, and nothing happens. That's not so bad when life is going fine. But when you've just been through a major setback—a flunked test, a wrecked car, a broken relationship, a death—you'd appreciate some two-way communication!

I've had the "silent treatment" throughout my prayer life. But it's only been lately, since I've begun thinking about prayer in terms of the friendship model, that I've allowed myself really to admit the *frustration* of that silence. Maybe you've felt it, too. You just want to yell out, "Why!" Why are you so quiet, God!"

It's more a cry of anguish than a question, more a whisper of hurt than a problem to solve, more an expression of loneliness than a theological puzzle. And that brings us back to *mystery*.

Maybe we can change our question *Why is God so silent?* to a better question: *What can we discover by entering into the silence of God?*

Let's return to the experience of human friendship. Say I've just poured out my heart to my friend, describing an argument I've had. It was an unpleasant scene, one in which I felt attacked by someone else and had to put up a defense against a lot of harsh words. There was little I could say or do. I'm almost in tears as I relate the incident, feeling again the emotions I felt during the argument.

My friend says nothing. She is just silent. And yet the lack of words doesn't bother me, because I know she is "with" me in a supportive way, a way that doesn't require words.

If I were expecting a response in words, I might be very disappointed. But we learn in friendship to set aside expectations little by little—and to appreciate that love is communicated in both words and silence.

My only way into the mystery of God's silence is to look at what kind of answer I'm expecting. I've read lots of stories about saints who've had visions, but I've yet to experience that myself. Nor have I met anyone else who has! And so I no longer expect a spectacular answer from God to my prayers—a *Star Wars* special-effects appearance a la George Lucas.

That kind of answer from God—a voice or a

vision or even an instant miracle—isn't part of my God experience. I am reminded of Bill Cosby's famous "Noah" routine. Noah is loading the ark while God gives instructions. When God complains that Noah is taking two female hippos on board and asks him to get a male hippo, Noah retorts angrily, "No—you change one of them!" God's answer is, "Come on, Noah, you know I don't work that way!" Behind the humor of the story is the truth: Noah might have expected God to do something flashy. Instead, God called Noah to set aside his expectations.

Discovering Richness in God's Silence

Very often, God doesn't work the way I expect, either. When God is silent, I have to look deeper: What can I discover in the silence? Perhaps I have to tune in to how God's voice speaks in deeper, richer ways. Here are the ways I have found:

In the Scriptures. Paging through a favorite book of the Bible (for me, the prophet Isaiah) often leads me to a passage that seems to touch the feelings of the moment. The Scriptures are certainly one way God "speaks" to us. Over the centuries believers have felt the power of these "inspired" words, that is, words filled with the presence of God's Spirit. God loves us in and through the stories, poems, prayers and teachings which are the family record of God's people.

In nature. Creation is another place to hear the voice of God. Once on a retreat I was overcome by sadness over a friendship which had ended. My prayer was full of regrets and even tears—but very few answers. I happened to be staying in a rural area, near some farmland. I decided to walk outside and wandered down a back road. Suddenly I found myself facing a vast field, just beginning to show signs of spring growth, with green shoots poking through the rich black earth. My mind was filled with images of hope. A field comes to life in the spring. Our lives can become green again with new life, new growth—even after a winter that seems to be full of death and endings. God's voice spoke eloquently through creation that day.

In other people. A fellow priest and I meet regularly to pray together in the silence of a downtown church near where we live. After our prayer time, we usually have lunch together, and our conversation often turns to what we were praying about. Once I recall saying something like, "You know, God really was quiet today!" That led to a discussion about my prayer. The silence of the "really quiet" God led to sharing between friends that must have been God's way of speaking to me that day.

In the silence itself. Sometimes the silence itself is an important gift from God. I've had the occasion to spend time as a hospital chaplain, visiting with people who were quite sick. Perhaps you've visited a friend or family member in the same circumstances. I always feel uncomfortable when I walk in the room. What should I say? How will the person react? What is he or she feeling?

Words seem to just fill the air at a moment like that. Usually *what* I say isn't as important as simply being there, giving a silent but supportive presence. I can't take on the sick person's suffering, but I can at least offer my presence. In our own moments of suffering, God's silence may offer us the same reassuring presence.

The movie *Tender Mercies* has a powerful scene

near the end which illustrates how the silence we experience in prayer can lead us through our questions to a deeper mystery. The central character, played by Robert Duvall, is a country singer whose life turns from disillusionment and drink to a simple peace with a widow, whom he marries, and her young son.

In the scene Duvall is working in their garden and recounting some of the tragedies he has known, and some of the ironies—why should his life be so good now when others suffer misfortune? He tells his wife, "I prayed and I got no answer."

His questions to his wife get no immediate answer either. She simply listens—the moment is too precious for a reply in words.

We began this chapter with the bittersweet comedy of Woody Allen, who captures in his irreverent, offbeat way some of the truth of loving. From his commitment to the frustrating yet crucial mystery of human relationships we moved into an equally compelling mystery—the silence of God. We end with another human story, that of *Tender Mercies*, which teaches us to honor that silence as a rich presence, full of loving.

But the mystery of friendship with God continues to raise questions for us. What about *answers* to prayer—something we've been taught to expect, or at least hope for? We'll explore that dimension of prayer in the next chapter.

Stop to Reflect

What does the word *mystery* mean to you?

Describe your reaction to a particularly moving event in your life, or perhaps to the grandeur of nature.

What expectations do you bring to your prayer? How do you expect to "hear" God?

How do you feel when God seems to be silent?

Something to Try

Experiment with silence. Spend some time in your room without a radio or stereo on. Listen for what you *do* hear. Try the same thing in an isolated spot out-of-doors. Take note of the sounds that you hear when you allow yourself to be silent.

Take Time to Pray

Set aside a prayer time and begin with a prayer of your own choosing. Then read a favorite passage of Scripture or some other selection which might help you to think about God. Then try to be silent, both inside and out, for a definite length of time—for example, five minutes. After that time, spend a few moments jotting down your reactions to the silence—what thoughts came to mind, how it felt. Use these reflections as a start for your next time of prayer.

4. The Machine Ate My Quarter

Getting Answers in Prayer

Quite a few years ago the Lay Franciscans, then known as the "Third Order," sponsored and produced a radio program called *The Hour of St. Francis.* The program featured weekly dramas which taught something about the Catholic faith in an entertaining and often humorous way. One of the most popular episodes was a story called, "What's the Trouble Up There?"

The story is a fantasy about a man named Joe Dokas who is always complaining about the way the world works. His gripes include the way God runs things: "I knock myself out praying and hardly ever see any results!"

Joe's complaints prompt a response. Heavenly officials send an angel to fetch him up to heaven where he gets a chance to take over the "prayer switchboard" and try his own methods of answering prayers. Joe—after he gets over the shock of traveling via angel—eagerly accepts the assignment. He feels he'll have no trouble satisfying people's prayer requests.

But trouble soon develops. Joe orders up a

medium rainstorm that he hopes will answer the prayers of farmers and fishermen. But roofers and racetrack owners complain that the rain spoiled their day! Then the farmers check in with the bad news that the rain did them little good. As the angry responses pile up, the angelic hierarchy decides to rush Joe back home. He's glad to go—having learned a lesson.

The story is funny and fanciful. Of course there's no heavenly switchboard. But oftentimes we imagine something like it as we pray for things we need and puzzle over the answers we get (or don't get) to our prayers.

Questions About Prayer

While writing this book I talked with a high school class taking a course on prayer. Their comments revealed a whole range of approaches to prayer. Some raised questions, questions which perhaps you've asked:

> There are so many people praying—how can God hear all of us praying at once?
>
> God knows what we think anyway. Why pray?
>
> How does "little old me" get God's attention?
>
> Is it just a coincidence when prayer for someone else gets answered?
>
> What if I don't get an answer—is it because I didn't pray hard enough?

Won't God—or others—think my prayer is just dumb?

The questions reveal a very human struggle with the problem and the mystery of prayer. And that's okay! It's natural to want to know how prayer "works." But these questions reveal something more fundamental than simply getting answers to prayer. Beneath them is that basic question we asked at the beginning of this book: *Is anybody there? Does anybody care?* Even if our prayer isn't the type which needs an answer, we still would like to know that *Someone* is listening.

Types of Prayer

To help us delve into this mystery, let's first look at some of the basic types of prayer.

Prayer of petition. The *Hour of St. Francis* story about Joe Dokas and his gripes illustrates one basic kind of prayer. It's probably the kind we're most familiar with. We pray for someone to get well, for a passing grade on a test, for good weather, even for the traffice light to change!

Prayer of petition is also the kind of prayer that generates the most problems. If you ask for something, you either get it or you don't. And if you don't get what you pray for or you get something you *didn't* pray for, that's a problem—or so it seems!

Not long ago I was discussing this kind of prayer with a group of folks and we came to the conclusion that while petition prayers may seem a little self-centered at times, we all pray them. They are very human prayers and for that reason we shouldn't look down on them. In their humanness they relate us to those we're praying for, and they keep us in touch with God. Even a frustrated prayer at the stoplight when you're in a hurry shows you're at least thinking of God. And that ought to remind us of the real purpose of prayers of petition—to help us put into concrete form our dependence on God.

But there are other kinds of prayer as well. Prayer can mirror the *many* ways we relate to God in a personal relationship.

Prayer of thanksgiving. Besides asking for things, we can also *say thanks*. This kind of prayer seems to come spontaneously when something good has happened. A successful school project, a good day at work, a fun evening with friends—all can be a springboard to prayer.

And the surprising thing about a prayer of thanksgiving, at least in my experience, is that thanking God about *one* good thing will almost inevitably lead to another, and another. It's a reverse on the old notion of "counting your blessings": In a prayer of thanksgiving, the blessings often seem to count themselves!

Prayer of repentance. When my relationship with God or others has been less than I'd like it to be, I may come to God with a prayer of *sorrow or repentance*. Most often, such a prayer can come from our experience of the human need to say, "I'm sorry," and be forgiven (contrary to the line from the movie *Love Story*, which falsely assures us that "Love means never having to say you're sorry").

I find it tough, though, to admit to another person when I've failed. With a friend, no matter how close or how deep the trust, there may be a lingering doubt: Will he still like me? Will she accept *this* ugly side of me? We can be sure that God will. The

Scriptures are filled with beautiful stories of repentance, and the forgiveness of God. The Forgiving Father and the Prodigal Son (Luke 15:11-32) is just one example.

Prayer of praise. And there are some times when we're just glad to spend time with God—prayers of praise and adoration. I'd like to suggest that we ought to give this kind of prayer its due. We're all familiar with the bubbly exuberance we feel during life's special moments—a great tennis shot (even when made by our opponent), the news about a friend's scholarship, the pleasingly nice feeling after the *first* piece of pizza, or the spontaneous release of *ahhhs* at a spectacular fireworks display.

Prayer of praise means simply bringing God into such moments. Praise means acknowledging that the beauty, the wonder, the joy of life is a gift of God.

Each type of prayer relates us to God in some way. How we pray in a particular moment will depend on our relationship with God.

But no matter what kind of prayer we pray, we may still wonder: How does prayer "work"? To help us understand that basic question we need to probe more deeply into the nature of our friendship with God.

What Do We Expect From God?

As I pointed out in the last chapter, if we are to grow in our friendship with God we've got to deal with the expectations we bring to this friendship.

We begin any friendship with expectations. We want it to go well. Remember the first date with that person you'd been waiting for months to meet? Remember the first day in class with the teacher everyone said was just great? Remember the excitement about meeting new friends in the neighborhood you've just moved into or the job you've just begun?

If any of those are familiar experiences, I'd be willing to bet that there's another memory that goes along. Your initial expectations usually don't match what actually happens. Have you ever set up the "perfect" evening of dinner, a movie and stimulating conversation over coffee—only to find a long line at the restaurant, miss the first five minutes of the film and discover afterward that the other person is too tired to talk?

As we get to know someone, we discover differences: She likes poetry, movies, square dancing and talk. He likes hiking, new wave, TV and can't make conversation well at first. Will it be a disaster that ends after one evening? Perhaps. But if there's "something else"—an attraction that goes deeper than superficial likes and dislikes—both will keep trying.

And even when I get beyond the surface features of a friend, there may be expectations that clash. Despite my best intentions, I might try to make the other over into *my* image of a friend. It's strange, but it seems to be the way with human beings that no matter how generously we start, there's always a tendency to make a friend into a mirror instead of a window; I want him or her just to reflect me, rather than open up new vistas.

All the same is true when we're getting to know God as a friend. Like the story of Joe Dokas, we may expect God to promptly respond to *our* wishes. Our visit to church or our time of prayer may be like putting coins in a vending machine. If I put in my money (pray), I get something from the machine (an answer to my prayers).

Does it sound silly? Perhaps. But I know at times I expect God to function that way. I get angry and frustrated at unanswered prayers. I get tired of always praying for things—for people to get well, for world peace, for the Cincinnati Reds to win ball games. My God, in those moments, comes perilously close to being more like a vending machine than a personal friend. And when prayers seem to go unanswered it reminds me of the times when the vending machine eats my quarters instead of delivering a Coke.

We somehow expect God to do all the work, to make our world perfect, to meet all our needs, because God is God. And yet like any good friend, like the Perfect Friend that God is, the greatest gift God gives is the gift of freedom. God lets us be free, refusing to force us to change, to make us love in return.

As with a good human friend, God will wait patiently for us to respond, to change. God never buys our friendship, never manipulates us. There is no master computer that doles out rewards and punishments, that drops airplanes out of the sky because the passengers are sinners, or gives a baseball team magic bats because the chaplain said the right prayers. To run the world on that kind of system would negate the freedom that God placed at the heart of it all.

And even though at first we'd like it to be that way, the more we think about both our human friendship as well as our relationship to God, we eventually realize that the way of freedom is the way we must walk.

So why pray? Maybe that's the *real* question,

even more basic than our concern with how prayer "works." It gets us back to where we started in Chapter One: *Is anybody there? Does anybody care?* Believing in prayer means believing Someone is there to listen, to give an answer. Believing in prayer means that Someone there wants to listen to *me*, cares about *me*.

The Real Answer to Our Prayers

Why believe in prayer? Looking at the types of prayer mentioned earlier can help us see why. Each type—petition, thanks, repentance, praise—spells out a particular way of relating to God. And once we begin to move beyond the very normal expectations we put on our friendship with God, we begin to see more deeply that each type of prayer expresses what any human relationship expresses—something "more" than we see at first:

There is more than an answer to my prayer of petition—there is the healthy sense of *dependence* on God who is the giver of all good gifts.

There is more than just courtesy in my prayer of thanks—there is the good news that God has first loved me, that God's love is a gift in my life.

There is more than fear of punishment in my prayer of repentance—there is *acceptance* from a friend who cares deeply, waiting for my return from being lost and alone.

There is more than just poetry in my prayer of praise—there is *joy and wonder* at the fact that God is at work in the world, creating beauty and goodness.

Prayer helps me get to know this Friend. After once meeting God, can I ever be the same? More profoundly than any human encounter, prayer invites me into the mystery of a love that can never be exhausted.

A New Way to See Myself

Dependence, gift, acceptance, joy, wonder: They are the result of friendship with God. And God uses these qualities to show me myself in a new light. The high school class I attended got me thinking about the ways we undervalue ourselves. Some of the students saw their prayer as worthless, wondering if God wanted to pay attention to them. It's easy to retreat into a whole host of put-downs about ourselves. And that doesn't do our prayer any good.

If we truly see God the way Jesus did, we come to acknowledge God as the source of all that we have. Jesus' own prayer addressed God as *Abba*, the loving Father who had shared all with his Son. In his teaching to his apostles Jesus stressed his relationship to his Father as one marked by openness, by an acknowledgment that all he had, Jesus had received from the Father as gift. And in Jesus' own prayer, the Lord's Prayer, we can see the acknowledgment of this giftedness, this relationship with God that he so much wants us to share.

If we see ourselves as gift, then we need never devalue ourselves again! An old banner statement of the 60's said it: "God doesn't make junk!" Although I've often said, "Sure, of course," to that statement, I keep coming back to it. Think of it yourself, and put it in the context again of human friendship.

Once when I was just becoming aquainted with a new friend, I invited her to look at an album of photographs I had put together. There were the high school plays I was in, my family members, scenes from some of the places I had visited. I hoped that by sharing the album, I could give my friend a better understanding of who I was.

But I almost blew it. Before I opened the album, I said, "Now, I hope you're not bored by this!"

My friend has never let me forget that put-down! And yet, don't we often come before God that way? We imagine God being bored with us, that we aren't worth the time, that we have nothing worth sharing. But if God has made us, then we're certainly not boring—we're important and significant. And prayer helps us to appreciate how we have been gifted.

Thus, our needs expressed in prayers of petition, our wonder voiced in prayers of thanks, our need for acceptance poured out in prayers of repentance, our dependence on the *Abba* of Jesus exclaimed in prayers of praise—all can be part of a healthy friendship with our God.

Think of your experience with your best friend: Does he or she look on you as merely a chance to practice being a good listener, as a supply of tears to be soaked up, as a willing depository of excess knowledge about trig? I doubt it. A true friend sees you, not as a needy vacuum to be filled (even if you have needs), but as a gift—to be cherished and nourished as a beautiful flower, with the blessings of sun and rain.

And so it is with God, I believe.

Still More Questions!

So where does all this get us? Probably to just more questions! But that's not bad.

A contemporary storyteller puts it well. Elie Wiesel, who uses his gifts as a poet, novelist and playwright to portray both the joy and suffering of the human family, wrote a play called *Zalmen, or The Madness of God*. The play is about a rabbi in the Soviet Union after the era of Stalin, who dares to speak out for the freedom of his people. Near the beginning of the play, a government official charged with keeping an eye on the affairs of the Jewish community questions the rabbi:

> *Inspector:* And you, Rabbi? Which side are you on? The questions or the answers?
>
> *Rabbi:* I am on the side of prayer....
>
> *Inspector:* What *is* prayer: question or answer?
>
> *Rabbi:* Both. Question for whoever believes he has found an answer. Answer for whoever struggles with the question.
>
> *Inspector:* Now we are getting into theology—I am lost.
>
> *Rabbi:* I pray in order not to be lost.

We pray in order not to be lost. Before anything else, prayer is a way of remembering who we are. In the face of all our expectations and frustrations, if we allow the God who is our friend to meet us in prayer and transform us, we shall never be lost. And that is a comfort, especially in the difficult moments of our lives. In the next chapter we will look at prayer in those moments.

Stop to Reflect

How have your prayers been answered?

What expectations do you have of God?

Which type of prayer do you like best? Why?

What does being dependent on God mean to you?

How do you express a sense of wonder before God?

Something to Try

Recall a special friendship you have. Think back to the first time that you met that person, trying to recall your "first impressions." Write down as many of those impressions as you can remember. Next write down how you feel about that person today. Do you notice any changes? Do you recall any expectations that have or have not been met? How has the friendship grown?

Take Time to Pray

The following psalms are examples of the types of prayer mentioned in this chapter. Choose one that you are least familiar with and use it as the basis for prayer:
     Petition—Psalm 4, 25, 27
     Thanksgiving—Psalm 30, 65, 116
     Repentance—Psalm 32, 38, 51
     Praise—Psalm 8, 111, 149.

5. Nothing But 'I Love You'

Prayer in the Tough Times

I have always had a tough time praying—except in the tough times.

All of us seem to be able to summon up some of our best prayers in those moments when we find ourselves backed against the wall by a crisis—a serious illness, a great loss, death. As one teenager told me recently, "You show your best faith in bad times."

A moment that stands out clearly for me was the unexpected death, not too many years ago, of a young cousin. The call came to the parish where I was working at the time that he had been found dead. My family, which is very close-knit, was all gathering at the house. Would I come right away?

Believe me, I did a lot of praying in the 15 minutes it took to drive there! I really needed to have God close by. I knew that as a priest I would be asked to function in my "professional" role—helping the others. But then I was also family and was starting the grief process myself. My prayer was a simple plea for help—one of those direct, honest prayers that seems to come from our "best faith" that God is near.

A beautiful response came to my prayer—although at the time I wasn't able to appreciate it as an answer. When I reached my cousins' house, the priest from their parish was there. As I came into the living room he came up and hugged me—saying without words: "Greg, you can just be yourself for a moment; I know you're hurting."

That hug symbolizes for me some of the feelings that I have about prayer in the tough times. In this chapter I'd like to try and raise some of those feelings and reflect on them.

I remember that the prayer I prayed on the way to join my family after my cousin died was full of confusion. I really did not understand what had happened or why. There were lots of questions.

Those questions at first centered around the facts of his death: how and when. But they soon moved into *whys*. And those "why questions" never really stopped. Even to this day I know my family still asks them.

Asking God those questions is natural! If I ask them of those around me, can't I ask them of God?

I may find myself demanding to know the answer to the why of a death or sickness. I may wonder why God didn't prevent such a thing from happening. I may wonder if somehow the tragedy was a punishment for something the person had done wrong. (Children—and some adults—even may blame themselves for a tragedy to someone close to them—"If only I'd been good to Grampa, he wouldn't have died.")

Who Is Responsible?

Jesus faced these questions on several occasions.

St. Luke's Gospel tells us that people asked Jesus about the deaths of some Galileans who had been killed by Pontius Pilate when they were offering sacrifice (Luke 13:1-5). Jesus reminded them of another incident—a tower collapsed and killed 18 people. In both cases, Jesus told his audience, these people weren't being punished because they were terrible sinners.

In John's Gospel Jesus faced the same question in the case of the man born blind (John 9). People wanted to know: Was he a sinner, or maybe his parents? Again, Jesus insisted that God doesn't mete out punishments in that way. God's love does not work in a petty or punishing fashion. God is not waiting to drop a piano on the bad guys who just robbed a bank; nor is God viciously picking out poor innocent victims and doling out tragedies. The misfortunes that happen are somehow part of the mystery of life and death that we all face. Jesus calls us to face up to what happens and to search out how that mystery can bring us closer to God.

And yet our immediate reaction—*why*—can leave us feeling discouraged at times. Some people just seem to have all the bad luck; others just seem to get the good. It isn't fair!

Asking *Why*

There are moments when the pain we are experiencing—our own or someone else's—gets to be too much for us. In the Old Testament a man named Job found himself in that position. He had lost all: his family, his possessions, but most of all the sense that he knew where he stood with God.

In the Book of Job we read some of the most

touching and honest writing in all of literature. Job cries out his questions to God, protesting that he's done nothing sinful. So why did all these bad things happen to him?

There comes a time when we all feel that way. Here's a poem that I wrote when those kinds of questions got to be too much for me:

Job-Questions

> Question pain for one who weeps the
>   hurting,
> Argue for the war-child's life;
> Seek solutions to a million hungers—
> Find no answers to this ache within.
>
> Walk for someone else the way
> Of fourteen different neat replies;
> Preach for each sad state the perfect sermon.
> (Can't my cross be stripped of mystery?)
>
> Questions traded, God and human,
> Innocent much more than me;
> Only waiting for one further question:
> Can you ask me in eternity?

We can begin to look at prayer in the tough times by asking ourselves what our feelings are in moments of difficulty—especially when someone we love is sick or dies.

If such a tragedy has happened to you recently, you may have clear memories; you may still be sorting out the feelings. Or maybe a close friend has experienced them and shared them with you. Think for a moment about your feelings and how you responded. That awareness will help us understand our prayer in such moments.

You may have heard of the work of Dr. Elisabeth Kubler-Ross. In researching the feelings of dying people and their families, she discovered that people facing a terminal illness or the death of a loved one go through a common cycle of feelings: They are often confused and puzzled—and may want to deny what is happening. They may try to make a deal with God or those around them—to "bargain" for more time. They may experience depression—and they often get angry at God.

When you discover yourself in such a situation, you may find these feelings affecting the way you pray.

Praying Our Complaints

Laying these complaints at God's door is a genuine form of prayer. Recall the complaints of Martha and Mary to Jesus in the Gospel of John: "Lord, if you had been here, my brother would never have died" (John 11:21,32). They were good friends of Jesus and trusted him enough to voice their true feelings.

I believe God is very open to hearing my complaints—as a good friend would be. No true friend would tell me not to feel the way I'm feeling. No matter if, in a more rational moment, I might figure out that God doesn't roll the dice and deal out punishments at random. When I've just heard bad news I may not be able to sort out what's reasonable. No friend expects me to; neither does God.

Job's complaints to God about the *why* of tragedies and misfortunes fill that biblical book. The fact that this great piece of spiritual writing has been treasured in our religious tradition shows that it both expresses a basic need of human beings—to ask God why—and enshrines a genuine form of prayer.

And what is God's answer to Job? Only more questions! In Job 38 and 39, God challenges Job to enter the mystery of creation and ponder its workings. The message almost seems to be: If you think you could handle the complexity of the world, you take over! Job backs down and apologizes to God for his complaints—but notice that the inspired Scriptures have yet preserved them for us in all the preceding chapters! Somehow, the deeper message of the Book of Job is that we need to enter into dialogue with God and confront the mystery of life.

I was surprised to hear a group of teenagers who had done just that express their feelings. We were talking about evil in the world. I guess I expected to hear a lot of confusion and complaints directed to God about why evil exists.

Instead I heard them say things like, "God didn't make hate, jealousy, war. God offers us peace....It's something we have to choose." Another comment was, "Why blame God for evil? We can do something about it. People are caretakers of the world. It's our responsibility."

The Answer Is Love

Nevertheless, neither you nor I would want to argue with someone who's just experienced the effects of evil. I trust that we'd react the way a good friend of mine reacted at a very difficult moment. His daughter had been killed the night before in a car accident. I came to see him the next morning, and since we were good friends I knew I didn't have to hide behind the mask of the "professional priest," someone full of answers.

I rang the bell; he opened the door. My first words were an attempt just to tell him how I was feeling: "What can I say?"

I'll never forget his answer: "You don't have to say anything except, 'I love you.'" And then we embraced without any other words.

"I love you" is what good friends can say without any need to give complicated answers to how the world works. God is waiting to say the same to us. Even if our prayer begins with complaints about the unfairness of it all, we need to remain open in our prayer to God's response in and through the mystery of our human experience.

Expressing Our Anger

Another important feeling—and perhaps much scarier—is the anger we feel in the face of tragedy and suffering.

We may feel that anger has no place in prayer and therefore try to bury our angry feelings. But buried feelings can be very destructive.

Facing feelings is healthy and necessary. You may know this already if you've experienced the death of someone close to you. One high school girl told me that after a family member died she was angry. "No one explained death to me," she said. She felt left out, treated as a child. But by the time she shared these feelings with me she was able to talk about them—she had learned the importance of looking at her feelings of anger and trying to understand them.

Are we willing to express our anger in prayer as well? A close friend of mine has worked with many families in times of trouble and has had the experience of listening to people's feelings without judging them (or worse, telling folks they shouldn't feel that way to start with!). This experience has helped her relate to God as well.

When a good friend of hers was quite ill, I promised to pray for him and his family. Through the weeks of his illness I listened as she told me how things were going. Often she felt angry: This sickness seemed to have no real reason; it was unfair. And she felt comfortable in telling God just how she felt!

Her prayer, an expression of hurt and frustration, brought her closer to God. One evening my friend gathered with other friends and family members of the sick man for a special prayer service at their parish. Those present offered expressions of prayer and support. Drawing on a wider community, these friends said, once again, the only thing we can say: "I love you." And they said it in the context of prayer.

Sharing Our Sadness Through Prayer

Prayer in the tough times *does* bring us closer to one another as well as to God. Rabbi Harold Kushner, who wrote the best-selling book on suffering, *When Bad Things Happen to Good People*, tells what it meant to him to respond to a request for prayers from a man whose mother was about to undergo surgery:

> By agreeing [to pray for her] I was saying to him, "I hear your concern about your mother. I understand that you are worried

and afraid of what might happen. I want you to know that I and your neighbors in this community share that concern. We are with you, even though we don't know you, because we can imagine ourselves being in your situation and wanting and needing all the support we can get. We are hoping and praying along with you that things turn out well, so that you don't have to feel that you are facing this frightening situation alone. If it helps you, if it helps your mother, to know that we too are concerned and hoping for her recovery, let me assure you that that is the case."

Times of deep pain and tragedy somehow let the gift of friendship—with God and others—shine through. When my father was very sick several years ago I felt so supported and blessed by the response of my friends. They became an answer to the prayers I was praying at the time; a way of God speaking to me the words of love.

'Blessed Are They Who Mourn...'

Priests have the happy privilege to share in people's lives at moments of joy—like celebrating the wedding of friends. One particular couple chose a special Gospel reading which they said expressed how they felt. It was the Beatitudes from Matthew's Gospel (Matthew 5:3-12). These words spoke of the blessings of the "reign of God": "Blest are the poor in spirit....Blest are the lowly....Blest too the peacemakers...." And I felt they were appropriate for a wedding. They seemed to be a nice "blueprint" for a marriage—a way to look at a life filled with many unknowns. My friends seemed to be saying, "We want to live our life in this way."

The words they chose were, of course, truer than they knew. Life is full of the unexpected. Later that year I heard with joy the news that my friends were expecting their first child. Everyone who knew them was happy and waited expectantly for the birth. During the time of her pregnancy, the mother-to-be found time to reflect on what having a baby meant; she wrote a letter to the editor of the local paper expressing what her unborn child seemed to be telling her about how all life was precious and needed to be safeguarded.

Then one night I got a phone call at three a.m. My friends' child—a little girl—had died as she was being born.

I hurried to the hospital. I arrived to share with my friends the sad moment of saying good-bye to their child, to cry with them, to do what we all do in such moments—just be present in love.

We met later to talk about the funeral liturgy for the infant. My friends had obviously prayed and thought a lot about what they wanted to do. They told me that they wanted to use the same Gospel for the funeral as they had used for their wedding: the Beatitudes.

Now, they said, they understood what those words of Jesus really meant: "Blest too are the sorrowing...." They knew that the mystery of life held both joys and sorrows and they still kept faith. They understood better now than on their wedding day that Jesus would always be with them no matter what happened, helping them to see even this moment of deep sorrow and grief as "blest."

The blessing did not mean dismissing all the hurt or covering it over with easy pious phrases. Rather it meant seeing honestly what their baby—even in the womb—had meant to them. She had affected their life together, she had even deepened their appreciation of how all life is holy. And she would always be a sign of the love they shared with their God.

It was a rare privilege to hear of such faith and to have the chance to tell others about it in the funeral homily. What makes the story special is not just the fact that it expresses faith in a moving way. For me the story helps to make the link between tragedy, friendship and what we must do in prayer—precisely what we've been talking about in this chapter.

These two special friends were willing to share their honest feelings with those of us who gathered around them at the funeral. They allowed the love we all shared to remind us of God's love. For me, that love began to answer my questions *why*.

Stop to Reflect

What questions do you have about evil or tragedy in the world?

What answer would *you* give to Job?

How do you feel about expressing angry or hurt feelings to God?

Have you ever felt supported in times of difficulty or tragedy?

What does it mean to pray for someone who is sick or dying?

Something to Try

The Book of Job is divided into several parts. There is an introductory part (1:1—2:13) which tells the story of Job's misfortunes. Then, in a collection of dialogues, Job's friends discuss his situation and he replies (3:1—28:28). In Job 29:1—31:37 Job makes a final statement of his case. A new character, a young person, arrives to provide an alternative viewpoint (32:1—37:24). Finally God speaks to Job (38:1—42:6) and the book concludes with the story of what happened to Job (42:7-17). Choose a section of the book that appeals to you and, after careful reading, try to imagine how someone from our time might express the same sentiments.

Take Time to Pray

Write a psalm of your own, expressing to God your hurts, frustrations or complaints. As a model, see Psalm 13, 22, 69, 77 or 88.

6. All Styles and Colors
A Sampling of Ways to Pray

Picking out a greeting card is always tough for me. To begin with, I'm not a big spender, so the price tag sets some limits. And then there are all those choices—comic, sentimental, bizarre. What's appropriate? Will the person getting the card like it? After all my head-scratching and figuring, I usually end up buying just one, even though I tell myself to stock up for those birthdays coming up.

Greeting cards are one way of communicating with friends; but they present such a variety of choices. You might say the same about prayers.

Prayer *styles*—the unique ways you and I pray—are personal. I may like quiet prayer before the Blessed Sacrament; you may find shared group prayer to be your preferred style. I hesitate to focus in on specific ways to pray—lest you come away with the impression that these few suggestions exhaust the possibilities. And yet a book on prayer ought to talk about some different ways to pray. Let me just add a warning note before I begin.

When I was in the seminary a group of people came in to give a prayer day for us. They were really sold on the charismatic style—expressive, spontaneous prayer with a lot of feeling. But their presentation made me feel that if I didn't pray the way they did, there was something wrong with me. I have never forgotten the bad taste that day left me with.

Your prayer and mine are different—period. My personality and history lead me to respond to the Lord in a way that's different from you. I'm glad it works that way! After all a flower garden, a meal or a circle of friends would all be boring if there were no variety.

So what follows comes with this brief "consumer's warning": Try what seems interesting to you. See what works. Adapt your prayer to fit your style. Don't be afraid to experiment. Let the ideas and suggestions of others influence your prayer life. Sample new styles. And be open to changing your prayer as you change and grow!

The Time and Place to Pray

Whether your prayer style is the rosary, an Eastern-style mantra, a formal prayer composed by someone else or silent contemplation, when and where you pray makes a difference.

To start with, the *time* of prayer is important. As with any communication with friends, you know when to call or visit—when things "click." Some parts of my day are better than others for prayer.

A lot may depend on your daily schedule, your style of life and whether you are a "morning person" or a "night person." I find it hard to start early unless I have someone expecting me to meet a schedule. I like staying up late. My prayer usually fits into that style.

On the other hand, I know people who can carry on complete conversations before nine in the morning! Amazing! Perhaps they also pray at that time!

One helpful thing is to find a time that fits. If you're a scheduled person (like me) or need a discipline for prayer (like me), you may find it helpful to settle on a regular time for prayer. That's always been hard for me, I must confess. It is a personal struggle to grow into a regular time for prayer. I try to challenge myself by the reminder that if I can set aside time for everything else (including some unimportant things), I should be able to do the same with prayer.

The *place* for prayer is another factor to consider. Atmosphere really affects your prayer. A place of quiet is essential. I also think that having a regular place, a place you feel "at home," helps your prayer to be more natural. Whether that place is your room, a favorite spot outdoors, a special church—choose it with as much care as you choose a place to spend time with any other friend.

A Comfortable Style of Prayer

The elements of time and place remind me that *familiarity* and *repetition* seem to help me to pray. Being in a place where I feel comfortable, using words that express me, following something of a pattern in what I do—all of these put me into a prayerful mood and make communication with God fit like a comfortable baseball glove or a good pair of slippers.

And that's how it should be. When you call a friend to chat, I'm sure you find a comfortable place to curl up with the telephone; you may find yourself laughing about the same old jokes or using an expression or phrase only your friends know. Friends find ways to feel comfortable with one another. Or, as a character in one of my favorite films, *The Return of the Secaucus Seven*, puts it, "It's nice being around people you don't have to explain your jokes to."

Perhaps that's why the rosary has never gone out of style—some folks find it just fits! They like the familiar words, the familiar images that come from meditating on the stories from the life of Jesus and Mary. It's not for everyone, but for many people it does have a comfortable feeling going for it.

I've found a related kind of prayer helpful for me. It is a personal phrase, short, rhythmic and easy to remember. On a retreat years ago a priest-friend suggested I compose a brief phrase that expressed my need for God, something I really wanted to say at that point in my life. I spent some time reflecting and praying about what I wanted to say, and then made up a phrase. Then I headed for the outdoors and just spent a long time walking, praying my prayer over and over again.

You might try it. It is really a simplified version of the Eastern "mantra," a prayer-phrase repeated over and over. The phrase should be something easy to repeat and meaningful to you, like, "Jesus, help me walk with you." I've found my prayer-phrase sticking with me over the years. Sometimes I vary it, change it to fit the moment. But it's become like a good friend—a prayer that rises up inside of me spontaneously. Again, it may not be *your* kind of prayer at all—but that's okay.

My prayer-phrase is also related to a more famous prayer style, one that I also like: the Jesus Prayer. It consists of the prayer, "Lord Jesus Christ, Son of the living God, have mercy on me, a sinner."

This prayer form originated long ago in the Eastern Church, and is often prayed in coordination with one's breathing. You can pray the whole sentence or shorten it—even just to the name *Jesus*, breathed in and out. This style of prayer is another form which uses repetition and pattern—a method many have found effective over the centuries.

Praying With Nature

As we saw in Chapter Three, one way God speaks to us is through creation. If you are fortunate to live where you can experience some of the beauty of the ocean, a mountain, the prairie or the desert, perhaps you have already learned to listen.

But there's "nature" even in a city bustling with life and activity. The seasons of the year mirror the cycle of birth and death, and teach us of the dying and rising of Jesus which is at the heart of our Christian faith. Each day's sunrise and sunset are psalms of praise and thanksgiving—if we will take a moment to stop and be silent. Even the beauty of the leaves of a houseplant glistening in sunlight can be silent prayer.

Try a "walking prayer." Find a time of day that will permit you some leisure. Pick a spot—a park, a city street, a country road. Ask the Lord to direct your thoughts as you walk. As you go along, try to look with new eyes at the passing scene. If there are people, entrust them—even strangers—to the Lord. If a beautiful flower or stately tree catches your eye, thank God for it. If you hear a song, a car horn, the bell of an ice cream truck, translate them into prayers that celebrate life.

Here is a prayer-poem from nature that I wrote

after a walk on a February day that seemed to promise the arrival of spring:

Some Small Hope

"Some small hope,"
I said
Where sunlight sparkled on the water
Through dry reeds,

Some small hope
Where brown grass
Hid the waiting green
Under my soft and sinking steps,

Some small hope
In the fresh spring-breathing breeze
That carried the thin high clouds
In a blue and shining sky.

"Some small hope,"
I said to God;
And it was my breathless
Question.

Using Scripture in Prayer

Earlier, I discussed Scripture as a place to turn when looking for God's response to us. (See Chapter Three.) There are many creative ways to use Scripture in prayer. You might want to start with the Psalms. They are the "prayerbook" of the Bible, a collection of prayers used by people of Old Testament times. They contain a vast selection of prayers for all occasions and situations—even though they were written in the distant past. And they are surprisingly honest (and sometimes startlingly vengeful!). These people were not afraid to express their frustrations with God in prayer.

You may have other favorite places to turn to in the Bible. Get an edition you can mark up and fill with notes. Begin your prayer-time with a Scripture reading or turn to the Bible when your thoughts wander. Use your imagination to put yourself in a scene: Imagine how it would be to walk with Jesus on the shore of the Sea of Galilee. What might he have looked like? What would you like to tell him?

One prayer method I like (suggested by two Jesuits, Armand M. Nigro and John F. Christensen) involves using one short Scripture passage, read several times. After each reading, write your reflections, share thoughts with others, or express a brief prayer. Each time, you may be surprised to find a development, a word or phrase that stands out differently.

Remember that the Bible is God's Word to us, a way to let God speak directly to us. The richness of the Scriptures has made it a source that never grows old or out-of-date. Besides, we have the presence of Jesus' Spirit working in the words of Scripture to teach us something new each time we turn to them.

Writing and Prayer

The prayer-poem above is an example of another kind of prayer-technique, the use of writing. Since writing is my business, I like to use it as a way of prayer. It's not for everyone, but perhaps you might explore it as simply another way to discover God speaking to you.

Lots of people keep journals as a prayer technique. Each evening they write something—a reflection of the day, feelings that have come, questions for themselves. A journal can be used for prayer by simply re-reading what's been written. Or you may try writing a prayer—one popular way to do this is to put your thoughts and feelings into the form of a "letter to God."

One thing that is helpful about writing is that it gets your thoughts *outside* where you can see them, reflect on them, even share them with someone else.

Here's a journal entry that I wrote while working as a deacon in a parish. In it I found myself moving from daily events to reflecting on how God was present and at work there. And that's the next step before prayer:

"A really good day! My CCD class, three strong, met tonight and seemed to go well: a really good feeling, perhaps some rapport built. I feel like we might be able to go with it…Now, to follow up on ideas, needs, dreams…

"Sharing with friars and sisters at the cookout earlier. Individual smiles, gifts…Truly a day of gifts. Almost forgot: Mass this a.m. with kids really enjoying song, sharing and the priest barking like a dog in the homily. Liturgical breakthrough!

"Thanks, Lord, for the small gifts, the unique beauty, the gentle teaching."

By the way—don't worry if your writing isn't Pulitzer Prize material. Remember that you don't have to show it to anyone except God. (After all, you may not be Lionel Ritchie or Sheena Easton but I bet you sing in the shower anyway!) With writing as with any prayer—just be yourself. It's what God likes about you!

Just Keeping Quiet!

There's an old story—I don't know where it came from—about a priest who saw an elderly man come into church each day. The priest was impressed with the man's apparent holiness from the way he looked as he prayed before the tabernacle. Curious, and eager to learn from the old man's experience of prayer, the priest approached him one day and asked, "Sir, you seem to have a beautiful style of prayer—can you tell me about it?"

The old man smiled and said simply, "It's nothing, really. I just come here every day, sit here, and look at him. And he looks back at me."

There's a lot of wisdom in that little story. Sometimes the best prayer is "just sitting." We can get hung up with trying to fill the silence with words. After all, our daily lives brim over with noise—music in elevators and "on hold," radios blaring, talk shows, headphones when we go jogging.

I want specifically to mention prayer before the Blessed Sacrament here. The Eucharistic presence of Jesus offers us a special kind of presence: nourishing, loving, promising to remain with us always.

I know that many times I feel guilty "just sitting." I feel as though I have to say something! Here's where we can take another friendship lesson. Two good friends can communicate a lot in silence—or, as Antoine de Saint Exupery's character the Little Prince put it, "It is the time I have wasted for my rose" that is important.

Try it with God.

Prayer With Others

Much of what I've said in this book is about the praying you might do by yourself. But there's a whole additional world of discovery when "two or more" of us get together to pray—as Jesus tells us to do in the Gospel (Matthew 18:19-20). There he promised a special presence when his followers gathered in a group. While prayer with others may seem a pretty big risk, I hope you'll someday give it a try.

Praying with your own peer group is tough, believe me. Even priests and religious are shy at this sometimes! It might be best to start with a very trusted friend. If you've talked about God or faith or other personal topics, you might have the groundwork for trying to share prayer.

I'll never forget one of the first times I prayed with a group of people. I experienced a great boost in faith when I heard an older priest offer a personal prayer that spoke of his belief and trust in God. It was sincere and honest, and has stuck with me through the years. Shared prayer is a gift from God I hope you get the chance to cherish as well. Your parish or school may have a prayer group you can visit.

And On and On...

I have only skimmed the surface of the prayer possibilities that exist. I haven't mentioned *music*, which is a stimulating doorway to prayer. St. Augustine is reported to have said, "One who sings well, prays twice." I don't know where that leaves us shower singers—but then, God's heard a lot, and if it's sincere...! A record, tape or instrument of your own can help enrich a musical experience of prayer as well.

Another aid to prayer might be a *special symbol*—a candle, a photograph, a polished stone, a leaf. Especially if the symbol was a gift from a friend, you might discover it leading you to remember him or her in prayer.

Praying other people's words also can assist prayer. The words of a poet can fill in the moments when our feelings and thoughts can't find expression, or when we need the talents of another to speak for us. Formal (printed) prayers can capture special thoughts other Christians, past and present, have found uplifting.

No matter what method or aid to prayer you choose, remember to keep coming back to the friendship model as a reminder that it isn't the style or the polish, the skill or the dramatic touch, the originality or the pizzazz that makes it prayer. Rather, it is the gift of love and time shared between you and your Friend.

Stop to Reflect

What style of prayer do you find most helpful?

Do you have a favorite place to pray?

In what ways can repetition aid prayer?

Does praying with a group enhance your experience of God?

Something to Try

Our prayer life can benefit from challenge. If you have always prayed a certain way, now may be a time to experiment. If one of the prayer forms in this chapter seemed interesting, try it out for a while. Ask someone to recommend readings on prayer. Find a trusted friend with whom you can regularly pray or at least discuss your relationship with God.

Here are some books you might find helpful: *Experiments in Prayer*, by Betsy Caprio (Ave Maria Press); *Anyone Can Pray: A Guide to Methods of Christian Prayer*, by Graeme J. Davidson with Mary Macdonald (Paulist Press); *Prayer, A Discovery of Life*, by Alexandra Kovats, C.S.J.P. (Winston Press); *Breakaway: 28 Steps to a More Prayerful Life, Experiencing Prayer: Three Settings,* and *You: Prayer for Beginners and Those Who Have Forgotten How,* all by Mark Link, S.J. (Argus Communications); and *Climbing the Mountain: A Journey in Prayer* by Mary Meegan, O.P. (Argus Communications).

Take Time to Pray

Father Bernard Basset, a well-known Jesuit retreat master and author, made a suggestion about prayer and gift. Observing that life itself is a gift from God, he encouraged his listeners to breathe deeply, take their pulse and pray, "Glory be to the Father, the Son, and the Holy Spirit!" It's just a start, but what a place to start—with the grateful acknowledgment that the gifts of breathing and blood pulsing are signs of the gift of life from God, and with a loving response of thanks and praise!

Epilogue

Do you remember the story of Jonah? He's the reluctant prophet, the guy who was happy to be on God's team until he got the assignment to run a play into the game when the opposition was the Assyrians, the toughest bunch of linemen in the Ancient Near East League where the Bible was written.

The Lord told Jonah to preach to the people of the Assyrian capital, Nineveh. He was to deliver the message that these rowdy folks had better shape up—or they would have to pay the consequences for their sinning.

Jonah got the message—and headed in the opposite direction. He caught the next boat for Tarshish, which was like going to New York via L.A. But God got the Word through regardless. With the help of a big fish, Jonah was delivered to Nineveh, where he got to work.

There are a lot more funny bits in the story of Jonah; you can read them in the biblical book of the same name. But beneath the folksy fun of this lighthearted tale is a deep and special message: *God loves us*, even enough to postpone the judgment day, cancel the fire and brimstone and turn a cowardly lion of a prophet into a believer.

    Here's my version of the story, filtered through the life of a priest, writer and pray-er who occasionally runs away from the friendship God keeps offering and of course—like all of us—discovers that God never, ever, gives up. It's a gift at the end of our short journey together. May you run into this friendly God along your way of prayer.

    Jonah-City

        I.
The mystery of loving is too much for me.
I'll take organizing the parish bingo
or setting up the schedule for holyweek or
anything but love.

I run scared from it.
I dodge life and hide away below deck.
I curl up and hope that I can sleep it off.

Oh yes; I can hear love's persistent call:
the patient waiting friends who (occasionally)
also yell at me
for being stupid and so
scared;
the frustration of flesh unvowed
(naively) offering love
from inside me;
the God who I know must be near
and (somehow) so very godlike
to be eternally loving even me.

And yet now I'm terrified—
frozen into numbness;

heading out of town to Tarshish
or to someplace
where there is not frightening
love.

II.
The mystery of loving is too much for me.
Its tearing, body-breaking gentle need
to give, to answer yes in some silence of death
is still a spark of life in this damp and empty
darkness:

An unheard-of surprise
party where I preached certain punishment,
contradictions to the neat plans I put around
the expected put-downs and the constant
sick stomachs of the rest of my life—
where a small and smiling face
holds all the dreams
I'd always wanted glowing forever and
where God
is nothing like I thought,
and more.

III.
O God
get me out of this crazy fish
that I might (un)swallow fear
and walk the much mysterious
loving which is for me.